The Journey Home

BY THE SAME AUTHORS

Julia C. Davis

Empowering English Language Learners, coauthor
Specialist Fourth Class John Joseph DeFazio: Advocating For Disabled American Veterans, coauthor
An Artistic Tribute to Harriet Tubman, coeditor
The Commission, coauthor
Finding A Better Way, coauthor
The Christian World Liberation Front, coauthor
Jesus among the Homeless, coauthor
Otto & The White Dove, coauthor
Letting Go, coauthor

Jeanne C. DeFazio

Creative Ways to Build Christian Community, coeditor
How to Have an Attitude of Gratitude on the Night Shift, coauthor
Redeeming the Screens, coeditor
Berkeley Street Theatre: How Improvisation and Street Theater Emerged as Christian Outreach to the Culture of the Time, editor
Empowering English Language Learners, coeditor
Keeping the Dream Alive: A Reflection on the Art of Harriet Lorence Nesbitt, author and editor
Specialist Fourth Class John Joseph DeFazio: Advocating For Disabled American Veterans, editor
Christian Egalitarian Leadership, coauthor
An Artistic Tribute to Harriet Tubman, coeditor
The Commission, editor
Finding A Better Way, editor
The Christian World Liberation Front, author
Jesus among the Homeless, coauthor
Otto & The White Dove, editor
Letting Go, co-author

The Journey Home

JEANNE C. DEFAZIO
Foreword by Julia C. Davis

RESOURCE *Publications* • Eugene, Oregon

THE JOURNEY HOME

Copyright © 2024 Jeanne C. DeFazio. All rights reserved. Except for brief quotations in critical publications or reviews, no part of this book may be reproduced in any manner without prior written permission from the publisher. Write: Permissions, Wipf and Stock Publishers, 199 W. 8th Ave., Suite 3, Eugene, OR 97401.

Resource Publications
An Imprint of Wipf and Stock Publishers
199 W. 8th Ave., Suite 3
Eugene, OR 97401

www.wipfandstock.com

PAPERBACK ISBN: 979-8-3852-2935-2
HARDCOVER ISBN: 979-8-3852-2936-9
EBOOK ISBN: 979-8-3852-2937-6

VERSION NUMBER 08/28/24

Scripture quotations marked NIV are taken from the Holy Bible, New International Version,*NIV.* Copyright © 1973, 1978, 1984, 2011 by Biblica, Inc. Used by permission of Zondervan. All rights reserved. www.zondervan.com.

Scripture quotations marked NRSV are taken from the New Revised Standard Version © 1989 National Council of the Churches of Christ in the United States of America. Used by permission. All rights reserved worldwide.

Scripture quotations marked NLT are taken from Holy Bible, New Living Translation, copyright © 1996, 2004, 2015 by Tyndale House Foundation. Used by permission of Tyndale House Publishers, Inc., Carol Stream, Illinois 60188. All rights reserved.

Scripture quotations marked ESV are taken from The Holy Bible, English Standard Version. ESV® Text Edition: 2016. Copyright © 2001 by Crossway Bibles, a publishing ministry of Good News Publishers.

Scripture quotations marked as NKJV are taken from the New King James Version®. Copyright © 1982 by Thomas Nelson. Used by permission. All rights reserved.

Many thanks to Kristi Lynn Martin who led me in prayer to receive Jesus as Lord and Savior.

Jeanne DeFazio

Contents

Foreword by Julia C. Davis | *ix*

Acknowledgments | *xi*

The Journey Home | 1

About the Authors | 41

Bibliography | 43

Foreword
Julia C. Davis

In Matt 28:16-19, Jesus commands all believers to fulfill the Great Commission:

> Then the eleven disciples went to Galilee, to the mountain where Jesus had told them to go. When they saw him, they worshiped him; but some doubted. Then Jesus came to them and said, "All authority in heaven and on earth has been given to me. Therefore go and make disciples of all nations, baptizing them in the name of the Father and of the Son and of the Holy Spirit, and teaching them to obey everything I have commanded you. And surely I am with you always, to the very end of the age.

Every Christian needs to share his/her testimony so others know why they received Jesus as Lord and Savior.

> I grew up under the influence of a Bible-believing mother who maintained that Scripture is historically accurate, inerrant, and fully authoritative as the Word of God. In daily prayer, my mother put God in remembrance of the promises in his Word. She believed that God "hath made of one blood all nations of men for to dwell on all the face of the earth" (Acts 17:26). I learned how to pray from hearing my mother cry out to the Lord. She pleaded with God for all humans to receive Jesus' gift of redemptive love and God's forgiveness.[1]

---

1. Davis and DeFazio, *Artistic Tribute*, 1.

Foreword

As an African American Christian author and educator, I am participating in this project because I believe that you can argue with a person's theology but you cannot argue with his/her story because it is what it is. These salvation accounts are a spiritual treasure. As I read them, I realize how varied and unique each Christian's personal experience of God's love, mercy, and grace is.

We are living in challenging times. If we speak up and let others know how we received Jesus into our hearts as Lord and Savior, we participate in the Great Commission and bring the lost to him before his imminent return.

> To accompany our brothers and sisters in all moments, but especially in the most difficult ones, is to practice the behavior of Jesus. He sympathized with the pain of others and offered the joy of the gospel.[2]

Exodus 14:13 commands Christians to "fear not, stand firm, and see the salvation of the LORD, which he will work for you today" (ESV). This prayer expresses my daily surrender, faith, and hope in Jesus: I will fear not, stand firm, and see the salvation of the Lord.

---

2 Reyes, Mathis, *Jesus among the Homeless*, 74.

Acknowledgments

Special thanks to Governor Jerry Brown for signing into California law the Workplace Religious Freedom Act and to Senator Jay Rockefeller for his support of The Religious Freedom Restoration Act in the United States Congress.

Thanks to Pope Francis for his latest book, *Life: My Story through History*. Thanks to Caleb Loring III and Peter Lynch for their kind support. Thanks to my beautiful niece, Ella Louise Ryan, who shares the love of Jesus with us all. Most of all, I thank Jesus for giving me the strength to carry on.

Jeanne DeFazio

The Journey Home

JEANNE DEFAZIO

Over fifty years ago, while we were both undergraduates at the University of California, Davis, Kristi Martin read Campus Crusade's "Four Spiritual Laws" to me and led me in the Sinner's Prayer to receive Jesus as my Lord and Savior:

- Law 1: God loves you and offers a wonderful plan for your life. "For God so loved the world that He gave His one and only Son, that whoever believes in Him shall not perish but have eternal life" (John 3:16 NIV).

- Law 2: Man is sinful and separated from God. "For all have sinned and fall short of the glory of God" (Rom. 3:23 NIV).

- Law 3: The only way man can reach God is through Jesus Christ. He died for us; through him you can know and experience God's love and plan for your life. "But God demonstrates his own love for us in this: While we were still sinners, Christ died for us" (Rom 5:8 NIV).

- Law 4: We must each receive Jesus Christ as Savior and Lord; then we can know and experience God's love and plan for our lives. "Yet to all who received Him, to those who believed in His name, He gave the right to become children of God" (John 1:12 NIV).[1]

This is the Sinner's Prayer I said:

---

1. Cru, "Four Spiritual Laws," 2–4, 6, 8.

> Lord Jesus, I need You. Thank You for dying on the cross for my sins. I open the door of my life and receive You as my Savior and Lord. Thank You for forgiving my sins and giving me eternal life. Take control of the throne of my life. Make me the kind of person You want me to be.[2]

Campus Crusades' "Four Spiritual Laws" were consistent with the orthodox Christian doctrine I held to be true as a Roman Catholic. I had memorized the Apostles' Creed as a child and understood the incarnation, Jesus as the Son of God and second person of the Trinity, and Jesus' redemptive work: his death on the cross for the forgiveness of sins for humankind, his descent to hell, his resurrection, and his ascent into heaven. In the Roman Catholic infant baptism ceremony, godparents, on behalf of the infant, reject Satan and embrace repentance to receive God's gift of grace to follow Christ's righteousness.

Since I had received the Catholic sacraments of baptism, communion, and confirmation, I said the Sinner's Prayer, expecting nothing to happen. At the close of the prayer, I floated home. I had a feeling of incredible joy. I never forgot it, and I always wanted to let Kristi know how grateful I was. Unfortunately, we lost touch as adults. I found her recently on a Dominican University alumni newsletter post. I was grateful to God that I was able to let her know before she passed how much it meant to me that she shared her faith and prompted me to say that prayer because it was a life-changing experience.

Sometimes we think we need to do more than is necessary to share our faith. Walking near a San Diego beach on the way to my mom's assisted living facility one morning, I turned into an alley to shorten my walk. I felt led by God to sing a praise song. In the past, when I sang praise songs in public, there were complaints (even though I would stop singing if others came near). I saw no one today in the alley so I sang. As I was singing, the voice of a homeless woman belted out a beautiful black spiritual while I continued to praise Jesus.

---

2. Cru, "Four Spiritual Laws," 10.

The woman's faith and love of Jesus was apparent in her singing. I looked around but couldn't see her. She was tucked away in a corner of the alley. I thanked God for her faith and prayed for her. I was so happy about this experience that I prayed that spontaneous praise and worship of Jesus, our Lord and Savior, would break out on the streets all over the world.

This chapter is a collection of highlights from the lives of precious Christian friends who accepted Jesus as Lord and Savior. I am so grateful they shared their testimonies of faith to encourage others.

DAVID GROFF

I'm glad you were able to reconnect with your old friend, someone who had played such a pivotal role in your life. As for me there were two pivotal moments in my faith journey. One was when I was baptized by total immersion in First Baptist Church in Sacramento at age nine. It was more or less expected of me by family and the church community, but it was still a profound experience that I have vivid memories of.

The second time came after years of agnosticism. When I suffered failure at Reed College, I decided I needed faith and I embraced God through Jesus.

One thing I didn't include was that my experience living in Africa first among Muslims and then among Christians helped rekindle my faith. Very few Africans in my experience are agnostics or atheists and nearly everyone professes some degree of faith.

That in a nutshell is my faith journey to date. Thanks for asking.

David

PS—A few years on a visit to Sacramento, I discovered that the First Baptist Church had dissolved. Sad.[3]

---

3. David Groff, email message to author, June 21, 2024.

The Journey Home
MARY CIARCIA

Happy Birthday in the Lord! I rejoice with you. He's sooo good!

I'm going to try to shorten this, because I went through more of a journey than you.

In 1974, I was teaching on a Navy base in Japan, and we had the same schedule as the schools in the US. A travel agency in Tokyo ran a trip to Taiwan for Easter vacation. I went. The last day of the trip was April 12, Good Friday. My best friend and I decided to go to the museum built by Madame Chang Kai-Shek to house all the treasures they took when they fled. We split up, and I wound up outside a tiny room. I felt I had to go in, and when I did, I saw some of the most beautiful objects I had ever seen—golden bowls encrusted with precious gems, ivory beads, etc., that were used in Tibetan Buddhist ceremonies by the lamas.

While there I had an encounter with Jesus, which changed my life. The mass became very special and I found myself talking to Him all day long.

I had no idea what had happened to me and had no way of learning. No internet. The only thing I could find were books on comparative religion, which I devoured. I settled on Christian Zen.

I came home about a year later and went to a church where I went to a retreat on Centering Prayer, sitting in silence with Jesus. From there, I went to a Charismatic prayer meeting, and from there, International Family Church. Hope this wasn't too long. I've never understood why he introduced Himself to me in such a way, but I'm so grateful that He did. I've stopped asking Him why, but will ask Him as soon as I meet Him at the end of my life. Enjoy the rest of this very special day. Thanks for sharing.[4]

---

4. Mary Ciarcia, text message to author, June 21, 2024.

The Journey Home
TERRY MCDERMOTT

I may have already mentioned this but I think I really wasn't saved until 2000 when I attended a 10-week Alpha course in Sacramento. Alpha is an introduction to Christianity from a Protestant perspective. It was time for the Lord to reign me in. During the course it was especially the women in the church who took me under their wings and taught me all about prayer. A couple of sessions during the course dealt with the Holy Spirit. For me it was beyond powerful. I was blessed at that time with what I call the gift of tears. Though it has diminished over the years, during worship and listening to praise songs—especially "Grace Alone" sung by Christina Hamilton—and during times of corporate prayer, tears would run down my cheeks. To this day I am not sure Whose tears they are. It was shortly after that that I attended a national prayer conference in Arizona. During a talk by a Pastor from Uganda, he stopped and turned on a dime and said: "God is watching America and the rivers of innocent blood that flow through her streets from abortion. Buckets full of tears need to be lifted up in prayer." Up until that moment I couldn't even spell abortion. God had a plan for me and I have been on fire for Jesus and for my call to stand up and speak up for those who cannot speak for themselves. Trying to defend the defenseless and be a voice for the voiceless is draining but until God takes this call away from me, I really have no choice but to do my tiny part and continue to speak and write about the ultimate civil rights movement of our generation. Shortly after being taken to my knees in Alpha, I had two experiences where the love of Jesus became shockingly real to me. Our church had an evening healing event. My wife went up to the front and a couple of church elders prayed over her. At that point in time I couldn't even spell "prayer." One of the elders, who subsequently became my mentor, related to me how when praying for my wife, he saw me sitting in a pew with my arms folded, not buying any of it. A while later I, as a baby Christian, was in a prayer circle with about 7 of the church's prayer warriors. I was so out of place. To this day I remember some of them on their knees, some standing, and some sitting. They were all pouring out their hearts to the Lord. I was way out of my league, but I knew then that I wanted what they had. They bore their souls with honesty and passion. Messy prayers devoid of piety and pride. Their authenticity broke me in two. God does indeed have a strange sense of humor. As time went by I became one the church's prayer warriors and wrote monthly prayer articles for the church publication.

These events taught me that God relentlessly pursues us and never gives up. Also, that it has nothing to do with our ability, just our availability. The second experience took place a year or so later outside an abortion facility in Sacramento. I had the privilege of being arm in arm in a prayer circle as our prayerful, peaceful presence stood as a testimony against what should not be. One of my arms was on the shoulder of Dr. Alveda King, Martin Luther King's niece. In response to my question she assured me that her uncle had been pro-life. It took me 50 years to figure it out. But as the Bible says, Jesus knocks at the door of our heart. The door handle is only on the inside. We need to open the door and invite Him in. If you do, you will never, ever be the same.[5]

BROOKS ALEXANDER

I felt that I had exhausted the possibilities of drugs, of meditation, mysticism, and the occult; I knew without taking things that far that there was no answer in the pseudo-values of idealism, intellectualism, and worldly success that I had experienced even before dropping out. The key to my despair was not that these various forms of commitment didn't deliver on what they seemed to offer ... it was exactly that they did make good on their promises, but left me, at the height of their fulfillment, feeling still blank and empty from the suppressed conviction

---

5. Terry McDermott, email message to author, June 21, 2024.

that something vital was missing—that there had to be more to life than I was experiencing.

The whole ambiguous and unsatisfactory story of my life came to a singular head one night in October, as I sat, stoned and alone, staring into a fireplace full of ashes. I saw inescapably what my situation really was. I understood that despite all the true things I had discovered, I had never come close to the truth. I knew that despite all the movement in my life, not only had I failed to arrive, I wasn't even really on the path. More frightening than anything else, I saw that I had gradually discarded the objects of my caring, one by one. I had begun with a concern for many things and large issues; I was left with the vestiges of a very small and self-centered itch of hedonistic ambition, and even that was perceptibly slipping away. I understood instinctively that when that was gone, I would have no real reason to go on living even for a single day.

Clearly, something had to change. Just as clear was the fact that the change had to be qualitative, and not merely quantitative (i.e., more-of-the-same-but-better was not good enough). As far as I understood what was happening that night (due mostly to the concepts I had absorbed from the Eastern religions), I thought that I was reaching down deep inside myself in an attempt to tap some positive source of energy that I visualized to be in there.

What actually happened seems (in retrospect) to be that God interpreted the whole situation as a prayer for help. The very next day, due to circumstances over which I had essentially no control, I was removed from the social context I was in, taken into Berkeley, and placed in the midst of an entirely new situation among people who were strangers to me. In that unfamiliar circumstance, stripped of my stale social expectations, I had the opportunity to see lived out before my observation, in a very visible and concrete fashion, a kind of caring relationship between real people that I recognized at once as The Answer to the anguish that I had wrestled with the night before. For the first time within my recollection I saw a style of life that I could honestly say that

I wanted for my own. I half recognized that the entire situation had been somehow contrived to confront me with an honest appraisal of myself and the appropriate antidote to it in the manner of a one-two punch, done so that I could neither avoid the issue nor misunderstand the nature of its resolution. I approached the people who were actually involved. They told me that what they had, and what I had seen, was—and came from—their savior, Jesus Christ.

At that point I did some pretty fast backpedaling in my mind. Almost instantly, a whole forest of false images and distorted concepts of Christianity popped into my mind, obscuring even my view of the personal reality that I had recognized in the first place. I had Jesus Christ well categorized in my mind—he had remained obediently in his niche for many years, and after all, I had transcended that narrow point of view long ago . . . hadn't I?

Those Christians were very tolerant of my groundless arrogance, and indulged my intellectual probings in a cheerful and willing spirit. For approximately a week, I hammered out the various conceptual issues to my own eventual satisfaction in a virtually nonstop conversation. I emerged at the end of that time recognizing that in fact I had become a Christian in the course of the week without being able to put my finger on the day or the hour. My Christianity seemed less a profession than a rueful admission, but I was joyful at what I had found. But in truth, I did not find the Lord; I wasn't looking for him. I was looking for a way out. When I had exhausted my own resources, he was able to find me.[6]

ARNOLD BERNSTEIN

I grew up in Queens, New York, in a conservative Jewish Family. Among my best friends were Tom and Frank. Both loved classical music, were Christians, and had

---

6. Brooks Alexander, email message to author, Mar. 29, 2022, quoted in DeFazio, *Christian World Liberation*, 20–22.

parents who were from Sicily. Frank, who had been raised Roman Catholic, had recently become interested in the Jehovah's Witnesses. I asked him to give me a New Testament to read, as we did not have one, and he gave me the Jehovah's Witness version. I was about sixteen years old, and, for me, receiving the New Testament—which I had always viewed as "the enemy's book" and absolutely forbidden—was scary. I read it with fear and trembling, feeling that I was committing a great, unpardonable sin, fully expecting to uncover great evil in it. I studied it in secret under the covers in my bedroom at night with a flashlight. I was mesmerized by the New Testament's description of Jesus Christ. This was not at all the person I expected to find as the central figure of Christianity. I thought I would discover someone who was ruthless, intolerant, prejudiced, and even militant—a lot like a few of the Christians I knew. Instead I found a model of faith, love, wisdom, and restraint. Under intense attack, Jesus conducted Himself with what appeared to be truly supernatural grace, wisdom, and love. In the accounts of His life contained in the Gospels, I could not find a single event in which He behaved in any way less than exemplary. Then I came to the accounts of His week of passion, betrayal, and crucifixion. Of this I was certain—no one ever lived as did Jesus. I was confronted with a major decision: what to do with Christ. . . .

Wrestling with the issues of truth is no simple matter. The more I struggled, the more frustrated I became. I was entangled in a web of conflicting ideologies, and I realized that, regardless of my effort, I might not be capable of discovering the ultimate truth of knowing God. This led to serious discouragement and a sense of futility. As a young man of sixteen, I was idealistic enough not to surrender to despair—but it was not easy. Often in exasperation I would wonder: If life has no ultimate design or purpose, why continue living? I arrived at a point of crisis when my need to discover the truth of God became all-consuming. I continued to study and win chess tournaments, and superficially appeared "normal," but beneath it all was an unseen maelstrom. Then a glimmer of hope appeared. I became aware that, though my desire for God was praiseworthy, my efforts to discover or experience Him were futile: it was not possible for me as a finite creature, through my efforts alone, to discover the eternal God. The only way I could find Him was if He first found me. My only hope was that, if I desired God enough, God in His love and mercy might reveal Himself to me. So I began praying, "God, if you exist, I beg of You, reveal Yourself to me." Because I was so impressed with the Gospels and the life of Christ, I also pleaded with most desperate intensity, "Enable me to know whether Christ is true or not." For a few days I continued, in private and with an abundance of tears to beseech the Creator to rescue me.

Then something totally unexpected happened. One day when I was alone in my bedroom, I very suddenly, as if from nowhere and yet also from everywhere, experienced a dramatic sense of the presence of God. It was much more than an inner warmth gradually building to a point of culmination. It was more like a flash of lightning coming from the pitch-black darkest night. It was sudden and overwhelming and I felt it at the core of my being. It is not possible to adequately describe the essence of this encounter. It was the living light of the presence of God. I did not merely think—I knew it was God. I knew it as clearly as I knew my own existence and the existence of the world. The presence communicated to me directly in an indescribable way, "I AM, I exist, and I am always here with you, at all times and in all places. Do not fear; I love you and always will." These were not words that I heard, but rather the sense of what was communicated. Also revealed was that Jesus Christ and the Gospels are true. What especially made this encounter with God real for me was that I can remember a specific point in time before which I walked, as it were, in darkness. Whatever thoughts, words, emotions, or prayers I said prior to this encounter were expressed in an atmosphere of darkness in which God was a distant possibility, not a presence. Following this dramatic encounter, the inner light went on and God became ever-present. The sense of His presence never departed and in fact remains with me to this day. I consider this to be my personal conversion to

Christ. I understand that many have not had such encounters. I don't think that everyone has to have such an experience. Some are raised within the Christian Faith and at some point claim it as their own; others convert from other faiths. In both cases, often the transition is gradual and not sudden. God in His wisdom chose this particular way to reveal Himself to me. For this I will be forever grateful. But I do not expect that everyone who desires it will have the same encounter. God deals with each of us uniquely.[7]

TED BAEHR

In 1975, God rescued me from the bondage to sin. I had begun financing independent movies for Canon Films when an older friend who had come to know Jesus Christ at the Billy Graham Crusade in New York City in 1957 suggested that I read the Bible to show her what was wrong with it. Reading God's word in order to refute it changed my perspective both professionally and personally. God rescued me. Suddenly, life made sense. Chasing after empty promises lost its appeal. Hedonism relinquished its hold on me by God's grace alone. There was no withdrawal from stopping the addictions, only the peace that comes from a personal encounter with Jesus Christ. Immediately, I was compelled to marry my beloved. The week before the wedding, a friend asked me if I wanted to accept Jesus Christ as my Lord and Savior and be filled with His Holy Spirit. I did. Filled with the Holy Spirit through my new faith in Jesus Christ, I decided to attend seminary at the Institute of Theology at the Cathedral of St. John the Divine.[8]

---

7. Bernstein, *Surprised by Christ*, 31–32, quoted in DeFazio, *Christian World Liberation*, 24–26.

8. DeFazio and Spencer, *Redeeming the Screens*, 5.

OLGA SOLER

When I arrived in Tennessee, I began a class called "Teachings of Jesus" by a professor named Robert Francis, who had been a lawyer, but was now a minister. His arguments were cogent and forceful. I put him through a lot of hard questions, but he gently answered them all. He was bringing me around with the help of the Holy Spirit, but I was not quite ready to give in. The denomination this school belonged to was very conservative. Not a peep of "Amen" or "Hallelujah!" was heard during service. Everyone wore their best clothes, and only hymns were sung. It was still easy for me to say, "I can get into Jesus, but this church stuff is a bore."

Then, one day, a black brother who had been convicted of murder, saved, and was paroled came to church and gave his testimony. Remember, I had been in the theater, did a little modeling as well, and now abhorred it when my nails chipped or I got a zit on my face. I dressed to the hilt and I did not like to look like anything but in vogue. But, when that brother started preaching, something came over me. I went to my knees when no one else was kneeling. Tears mixed with mascara rolled down my face like mud. I sobbed from deep in my chest and could not breathe. The preacher was weeping too and telling us how he had been a "filthy, nasty, dirty sinner," but Jesus had made him clean. I wanted that: he was talking to me. When he called for people to come forward, a few hesitant souls walked up, but I had to crawl. Everyone stared, but I was beyond embarrassment. I needed Christ, and I did not care who knew about it. I did not care what I had to do to get him in my life.[9]

SUSAN STAFFORD

At thirteen, I had gone to the Billy Graham Crusade in Kansas City on a Baptist church bus trip. I took my walk up the aisle and gave my life to the Lord. More than

---

9. DeFazio and Spencer, *Redeeming the Screens*, 40.

twenty years later, I was a syndicated radio broadcaster with the McLendon radio stations and interviewed Hal Lindsey, author of *The Late Great Planet Earth*. Hal suggested I find a church, so I began attending Pastor Jack Hayford's Church on the Way. As an adult, and understanding more about the Lord, I recommitted my life to Him on May 7, 1972.

I began hosting Bible studies in my home for Rev. Kenn Gulliksen, which evolved into what is now The Vineyard. This was my introduction to born-again Christians (Gavin and Patti MacLeod, Pat and Shirley Boone, Billy Davis Jr. and Marilyn McCoo) who have become lifelong friends. Rev. Bob Reith of Media Fellowship International baptized me in the Jordan River in the early 1980s....

I lived a life of self, and my "self" died. God placed a call on my life, and I have found great satisfaction in serving the Lord Jesus Christ.

Life on earth is, in essence, an introduction to eternity. When we do not know Jesus, we make choices as though there is no afterlife. In reality, how we live in this life determines our eternal state. I understand from personal experience that earthly accomplishments have no value in my gaining eternal life. My highest social or civic honors will not earn me entrance into heaven. Speaking from personal experience, I explain often what it is like as a Christian to take up my cross daily and follow the saints who have preceded me.

I mentioned that my childhood left me with abandonment issues that took a lifetime to work out. I have learned to view life from an eternal perspective and find value because I am loved and accepted in my beloved Jesus, whose love has brought the greatest emotional healing in my life. The experience of being accepted in the Beloved, which Paul expresses in Ephesians 1:6,[10] reminds me constantly of the wonderful kindness God has poured out on me because I belong to his dearly loved Son, Jesus. God brought me into unmerited favor

---

10. "To the praise of his glorious grace that he bestowed on us in the Beloved" (NRSV).

through Jesus's death and resurrection and made me the object of his grace and mercy.[11]

BOB YERKES

While with Ringling Brothers Circus, I decided to read the Bible. I grew up with a blind Christian aunt who possessed great spiritual insight, and her belief in Jesus impacted my early life, though I was reared in an unbelieving home. As a young adult, I have to confess I read the Bible planning to denounce the truth of it, but I realized that it had to be inspired by God.

Steve Terrell, the oldest son in the television series Life with Father, took me to the Village Church in Burbank, California. At 25 years old, I became a believer. I formed a group at Ringling Brothers Circus to read and study the Bible. I got my two friends, Reggie Armour and Bill Snyder, interested, and the first Bible study meeting was held in Little Rock, Arkansas. The group was nondenominational, including Roman Catholics as well as Protestants. My pastor, Reverend Phil Gibson, sent literature to help us in our worship.[12]

MEL NOVAK

I was blessed with a praying Christian mother. When I was a child, the medical prognosis was that my leg would have to be amputated. Through the prayers of my mother, God miraculously healed my leg. Her faith influenced my life deeply. My faith in God grew as I experienced a series of injuries that were miraculously healed. A native of Pittsburgh, Pennsylvania, I was an outstanding athlete in several sports who passed up sixty football scholarship offers to sign a pro-baseball contract with the Pittsburgh Pirates. My career was cut short by a massive rotary cup

---

11. DeFazio and Spencer, *Redeeming the Screens*, 48–49, 51.
12. DeFazio and Spencer, *Redeeming the Screens*, 57.

tear. Through prayer and very challenging rehabilitation therapy, my rotary cup tear healed. I endured ten failed surgeries on my throat in ten years, and, once again, the example of my mother's deep faith and prayers encouraged mine, resulting in each miraculous healing. I look back now and realize that, through every infirmity, God gave me healing after healing that encouraged my faith in him.[13]

APRIL SHENANDOAH

My precious grandmother always told me to put God first; however, I did not understand what she was telling me, since I already believed in God. Life's distractions tended to get in my way of living for God. I was living for myself during the week and giving an hour or two to God on Sunday. That is how I lived for years. Then, it seemed everywhere I went, I started hearing, "Seek first the kingdom of God." While I was attending different prayer groups, someone would invariably say to me, "Seek first the kingdom of God." It didn't stop! One evening, while visiting my friend Rita Seiffert (founder of Women of the Valley in Las Vegas), I once again heard those words from Matthew 6:33. In the early 1980s, as I was watching the *700 Club* on CBN (Christian Broadcasting Network), I felt like lightning came through the roof and zapped me. I gasped a deep breath and started weeping, literally sobbing for what seemed like hours. When I stopped crying, my first thought was, "That's what Gramy meant." Put God first; seek the kingdom of God first! In that instant, I thought differently and saw myself from a brand new perspective. That was the beginning of the greatest adventure of my life. The biggest change came when I told God from my heart, "I don't want what I think I want anymore; I want what you want for my life. I surrender my life to you!" The second was when I was baptized in the Holy Spirit with the evidence of speaking in tongues in the late 1980s.

13. DeFazio and Spencer, *Redeeming the Screens*, 74.

A woman named Louise French prayed every week at our prayer group that I would receive the gift of tongues. I did not know much about it, but said that I was open to it if God wanted me to have it. Week after week, she continued to pray with no results. Then one day, while I was driving home after she had prayed for me, up out of my belly and out of my mouth came a different language. I could not stop speaking for quite a while. It put me on a high like I had never known. With the gift of tongues came the hunger for God and his word. After that, my life took on new meaning: answered prayer, healing miracles, divine encounters. God's provision and great favor were occurring on a regular basis.[14]

GEMMA WENGER

I was born to Raymond John Wenger Jr., a brilliant Harvard Law School graduate who had a heart to become a priest. When the priesthood did not materialize, he instead married a Protestant woman from Kansas, Beulah "Bee" Beyer. Beulah had left the Midwest for California to be with my father and eventually became a celebrity cooking show television host. Through various real-estate investments, my parents were finally able to purchase a modest home in a nice neighborhood in Los Angeles.

From a young age, I was groomed by God. My father, being a godly man, led me to the Lord when I was three years old with the promise that "presents" would ensue. He encouraged my sister, Lisa, and me to pray for an hour a day, and he, being Catholic, faithfully took us to daily Mass. I remember my sister and me lying with my dad on the big king-sized master bed with the gigantic orange velvet comforter and him telling us all about Jesus. He said that, if we asked Jesus into our hearts, then we would get presents. I said, "Oh, yes, I want that." My father led me in the sinner's prayer, and I remember the feeling I had at such a young age when Jesus came into

---

14. DeFazio and Spencer, *Redeeming the Screens*, 102–3.

my heart. I specifically remember asking my dad, "Where are the presents?" My dad responded, "They are coming, you will see. They don't come all at one time, but they will be here." I remember having a feeling of disappointment at not having actual presents, but God gave me a vision of presents in my head. I saw them in the Spirit. I can still see that exact same vision in my mind today that I had many years ago. I have seen the gifts of God in my life, and I do praise God for all of his miraculous wonders that he has done throughout the years.[15]

CHARLENE EBER

In the early 1980s, veteran actress Joan Caulfield found an advertisement for Video Ventures in the Los Angeles telephone book. She contacted Hollywood director and producer Charlene Eber from that advertisement at the request of her longtime friend, Michael P. Grace II. Mr. Grace, a former Broadway producer and the chief executive officer of Grace Motion Pictures, asked Charlene to film a ministry event for Breath of the Spirit, the international Christian ministry of Michelle Corral and her mother, Joanne Petronella.

Charlene's husband, Ken, asked Joanne to pray for Charlene, who was dying of cancer. One night, Charlene had a life-changing experience. She knew at that moment that Jesus had healed her. After her medical reports evidenced the miraculous recovery, Charlene recalls walking through the University of Southern California (USC) Hospital wondering why people in the hallway were applauding. She thought perhaps there was a Hollywood movie star passing by, and then she realized that the staff was cheering for her for a miraculous recovery that defied the understanding of modern science and medicine.

Charlene grew up in a Roman Catholic home where she knew and loved Jesus, but her life-changing and miraculous healing from terminal cancer gave her

---

15. DeFazio and Spencer, *Redeeming the Screens*, 116–17.

relationship with Jesus a new start. Her personal experience of Jesus's healing touch allowed her to understand at the depths of her heart and soul the extent of God's mercy and love. Her answered prayer opened up a way for her to live her life more completely for Jesus.[16]

LARRY ABERNATHY

My name at birth was Larry Duane Jaggers. My parents were married early and soon divorced. I came under the care of my aunt and uncle. During the Great Depression, they were unable to provide for me and placed me as a young child in a Baptist orphanage. I was born during my father O. L. Jaggers's profligate years. From the time I was a small child, I have recollections of my dad, O. L. Jaggers, as an amazing pianist and singer. He played guitar and several other instruments. As a young man, he traveled all over the United States preaching, singing, and playing instruments as well as his famous collection of antique glass goblets, which he also played as instruments. In his book, *How God Gave this Ministry to Me*, O. L. tells how his musical talents took him out of the church into the world of secular music. He formed a swing band, which led him to immense popularity at the age of eighteen. For five years, he reports, he turned to the beggarly elements of sin; he started to drink and eventually became discouraged with success. O. L. visited his parents, who had never stopped praying for him, and gave his life back to Jesus, knowing that he was called to preach and sing the gospel.

In 1942, when I was five, O. L. Jaggers came and took me out of the orphanage in Oklahoma City for a special weekend that changed my life. I heard him preach Scripture and heard each word of Acts 2:17 as if it were written directly to me: "And it shall come to pass in the last days, says God, that I will pour out of my Spirit on all flesh; your sons and your daughters shall prophesy, your young men shall see visions" (NKJV). I told my sister

---

16. DeFazio and Spencer, *Redeeming the Screens*, 128.

who was in the orphanage with me that this prophecy was about me. (This sister is the daughter of my adopted parents, not my biological sister, Joan Jaggers Morton.) On that day, I was filled with the Holy Spirit. At the age of eight, I was baptized in water and had a vision of Jesus calling me to ministry. I could not understand why everyone in the Baptist Home for Children could not understand this.[17]

LEAANN PENDERGRASS

I grew up in Fort Payne, Alabama, a town with a population at the time of approximately eight thousand. When I was eleven years old, the minister at the Lebanon Methodist Church in Fort Payne asked if anyone wanted to receive Jesus and join the church. I lifted my hand and made a decision to accept Jesus as my Lord and Savior and to join the Methodist Church. I became a believer whose salvation was secure and a faithful churchgoer. But, when I turned twenty-three, I realized that I needed to know the Lord better. I would wake up in the night to pray and seek God for my future.

In 1992, one morning at 2:00 a.m., on the steps of a church in Mobile, Alabama, I was seeking Jesus in prayer. I asked the Lord to speak to me through Scripture and was reminded of Jesus's words in Eph 4:11–12: "The gifts he gave were that some would be apostles, some prophets, some evangelists, some pastors and teachers, to equip the saints for the work of ministry, for building up the body of Christ" (NRSV). John 15:18–19: "If the world hates you, remember that it hated me first. The world would love you as one of its own if you belonged to it, but you are no longer part of the world. I chose you to come out of the world, so it hates you" (NLT).

I wept as I prayed, understanding that God had chosen me to come out of the world to serve him. Then, I was filled with the Holy Spirit and started to speak in a heavenly language, according to Acts 2:1–4. On the

---

17. DeFazio and Spencer, *Redeeming the Screens*, 160–61.

day of Pentecost, seven weeks after Jesus's resurrection, the believers were meeting together in Jerusalem. "Suddenly from heaven there came a sound like the rush of a violent wind, and it filled the entire house where they were sitting. Divided tongues, as of fire, appeared among them, and a tongue rested on each of them. All of them were filled with the Holy Spirit and began to speak in other languages, as the Spirit gave them ability" (NRSV). I started to receive greater revelation from the Word of God. The Lord gave me John 15:16: "You did not choose me, but I chose you. And I appointed you to go and bear fruit, fruit that will last, so that the Father will give you whatever you ask him in my name" (NRSV).[18]

LINDA HENRY CHAPMAN

Two times in my life when I asked the Lord into my heart as my Savior I was lifted above my body into a heavenly place of amazing beauty, energy, and perpetual love not known in this earthly body. The first time, I was 8 years old when a Billy Graham crusade was on TV. He asked all who wanted to receive Christ as their Savior to say this Prayer . . . I was compelled to say it from my heart. My spirit went above my body, and I could still see and hear my family in the room who were behind me, as I was sitting stoic on the wool woven rug in front of the TV. It was as if I was going through the TV to where the crusade was, yet I was still in the TV parlor as I repeated the prayer Bill Graham said. Afterward, I went immediately back into my body full of indescribable love, joy, peace, and faith.

The second time I received Christ was in Acapulco, Mexico. I was 21 and, for a few months, living a life full of adventure, doing TV shows, and photo sessions. I was put into several magazines. I did modeling jobs, went to movie premieres, etc. I was not going to church or praying. Life was exciting, yet I felt so dead inside. The "F" was in everyone's language expression, and I started

---

18. DeFazio and Spencer, *Redeeming the Screens*, 143–44.

using it in a vulgar way. This is a word that I first heard when inmates drove by me when I was 12 years old, riding my horse. It defiled me, piercing and hurting my heart. I rode my horse up to the house. Telling my mama what happened. She replied, "Don't ever say that word again. It is a very bad word!" Yet, I was saying it now as a 21-year-old young lady. I walked away from my friends on the beach, crying out to God, "Lord, have I been so rotten that you have left me? I feel so dead inside. Have I lost you forever? Please, Lord, forgive me and give me a sign that I know you are back in my life! I want and need you, Lord!"

Bam, I went face forward like a flat ironing board into the sand. My spirit rose above my body. The Lord spoke to me, "My precious child, you have received my salvation, and again have asked for forgiveness, go and walk in my spirit and live by my word. You have eternal life." I argued, "Lord, I want to stay here with you in this perpetual Love, Joy, Peace. I want to stay here!" The Lord repeated, "Go walk in my spirit and live by my word. You have eternal life. You have work to do for me on earth!" Three times, I argued, wanting to stay with the Lord in this heavenly place.

While I saw and could hear my friends yelling for me to get up, calling out, "Linda, are you OK? Get up!" Another one asking, "Is she dead?" As soon as my girlfriend started to put her hand on my shoulder, bam, I was back into my body. All I could say to them was, "I'm fine," as I struggled to get up. In the remaining days in Mexico, I felt like I was living in a bubble of light, and several strangers remarked that I had such a glow upon me. That was my renewal into serving and seeking a closer relationship with Christ's anointing. Phil 1:21 recognizes and rebukes the nature of the flesh. You gain in Christ supernatural divine wisdom, true fellowship, anointed worship, pure righteousness, and a real Holy Spirit energy empowerment authority. Amen, rejoice.[19]

---

19. Linda Henry Chapman, text message to author, June 24, 2024.

The Journey Home

WILLIAM DAVID SPENCER

My arrival at college a month late, wan and weak from a physical illness, with no safety net provided, meant I had to lock down, playing catchup for a semester. At the first convocation held in the Old Queen's quad, our college president advised us to look to our left and then to our right, because at graduation two of us would not be there. I decided I was not going to be one of those two. He was right. The freshman on my left discovered he had impregnated his girlfriend as his goodbye gift and was ordered by both sets of parents to drop out for a permanent hello and marry her, which he did. The one on my right, who became a good friend, turned out to be laboring under impossible demands placed on him by his single mother and aggressive aunt who lived with them, demanding he travel back each week to another state to help rear his younger siblings. He soon attempted suicide and was locked away in an asylum. I visited him there, encountering the aunt who heaped all the blame on his lack of empathy for his mother's plight. I was bereft of both my new friends before the first semester ended. Rutgers New Brunswick was an all-men's college at the time and, once I had secured myself as a student, I naturally wanted to meet women. My mother kept telling me InterVarsity Christian Fellowship was the place to go. I was not interested in going back to a Christian group. I held off as long as possible. Then, since nothing else was working (and I loved my Mom, my parents and I being close, since I was the only surviving child), and basically to shut Mom up, I gave in. Mom was right. I met the love of my life, Aída Besançon, in the Rutgers Douglass IVCF fellowship. I write this afterword, by the way, in June of our fiftieth year of marriage.

What I found in Rutgers InterVarsity were serious young men, many upperclassmen, with whom I could identify and whose lives glowed with Christ. What I had heard all my life in church was actually alive right in front of me. I didn't learn anything new. I just saw something vibrantly alive that I hadn't caught yet. I also found a whole treasury of remarkable women at nearby all-women's Douglass College.

As a result of my decision to follow Jesus seriously, I took this commitment to heart, heading out on the streets of my birth city, Plainfield, New Jersey, on weekend nights, handing out Moody science Bible tracts, which I considered at that time the most attractive tracts available.[20]

AARON EZRA MANN

Aaron Ezra Mann received Jesus as Lord and Savior from an orthodox Jewish background:

> German-born American producer, writer, and director Aaron "Ezra" Mann is most probably best known for co-producing *In the Region of Ice*. This motion picture won an Academy Award (Oscar) for the best short live-action drama of 1977.
>
> With the birth name of Icek Jakob Fiszmann, Aaron's life has been enriched with a theatrical family legacy spanning well over a century! His aunt Dora Zlotnik was a popular Polish silent-film screen actress. Her career started when she was cast as an extra in Charlie Chaplin one-reelers. Miss Dora (stage name) toured across Europe's most beloved opera houses and cabarets, performing live her unique Vaudevillian style of song and dance. Fortunately, Aaron's parents did survive the war (in spite of stints in German internment camps). His mother, Jean, was born in the small town of Sosnoweicz. Her father, Ruben Zlotnik (Aaron's grandfather), was an Orthodox Jewish rabbi from the highly regarded family the Zlotnik rabbinical dynasty. Ironically, this particular area of Poland was also home to the future who's who of Hollywood, such as Louis B. Mayer, Harry and Jack Warner (Warner Bros.), Myron Selznik, Adolf Zucker, Paul Muni, Pola Negri, and Schmuel Gelbfisz (later changed his name to Samuel Goldwyn). Aaron's father, Samuel,

---

20. DeFazio, *Christian World Liberation*, 88.

was also born in Poland in the larger city of Lodz, which is the birthplace of Roman Polanski. The nearby city of Warsaw was home to Film Polski, where Roman attended. At that time, Film Polski was considered by many to be the world's finest film school.

    After the war, Aaron's father apprenticed as a projectionist/cutter for Central Film Productions in Munich, Germany. Central specialized in the making of company training, military, and institutional films. Samuel later became one of Germany's most sought-after theatrical film producers.[21]

After Aaron received Jesus as His Lord and Savior, he ministered in Hollywood to bring the lost to Jesus:

> In the early to mid 1980s I assisted Evangelist Ada Schwartz who was ministering in the small chapel at the well-known Presbyterian Church in Hollywood, California. The Hollywood Presbyterian Church was the home to celebrity Pastor Lloyd Ogilvie, who later served as chaplain to the U.S. Senate. These meetings attracted an assortment of homeless, marginalized individuals from the neighborhood. One such homeless man, Mike, had graciously volunteered to play an old upright piano during worship and played like a true professional. Mike was wonderful! The crowd was quite "eclectic" with members of Hell's Angels, prostitutes, streetwalkers, drug users, etc. All were blessed by the outpouring of the Holy Spirit[, all] who were drawn in through the heartfelt praise and worship; not to mention the giftings of Ada Schwartz. Many received Jesus as their Lord and Savior at› those services. A very kind, likable man by the name of Jimmy, and benefactor to Ada, strummed an anointed guitar and often accompanied her. Jimmy also provided various snacks for everyone with leftovers always given to Mike. After serving under Ada's ministry a number of years, the Lord blessed me with my own ministry at His House Ministries. The meetings were held at the Beverly Hills home of a former child movie star from Japan, who

---

21. Aaron Ezra Mann, email message to author, February 8, 2021, quoted in DeFazio, *Finding a Better Way*, 12–13.

later became a Hollywood movie producer. In his unique, loving style the Lord brought some of the same "eclectic" people from years earlier at the Hollywood Presbyterian Church to His House. Truly amazing! Once again the precious Holy Spirit was at work blessing us. Many were delivered and set free . . . but this time in Beverly Hills.[22]

YVONNETTE O'NEAL

God in his infinite wisdom develops cross-cultural Christian community to edify the church. God has used Yvonne's personal history, social skills, and spiritual gifts to break down the walls of prejudice and build cross-cultural Christian community. As an African-American child, at the height of the civil rights movement in Mississippi, Yvonne was integrated into all-white schools. This experience taught her to relate to the individual independent of race, color, or creed. In Southeast Washington, DC, as a young adult on staff at the Frederick Douglass Center and the Fishing School, her ethnic background gave her the education and social skills necessary to teach the predominately African-American inner-city students how to develop in order to succeed in a multicultural society.

In the late 1990s, Yvonne was a liaison for a Southeast DC Arts program developed through the Little White House in the Southeast Washington, DC. Networking with many Christian artists and philanthropists from diverse cultural backgrounds, the Little White House in the Southeast DC neighborhood set high standards that helped break cultural barriers and promote multicultural community. The added component of the love of Jesus embodied in the soul, spirit, and visual expression of the Christian artists who participated in that program provided a spiritual depth that benefited the adults and children of the Southeast DC neighborhood. This project modeled God's development of cross-cultural Christian

---

22. Aaron Ezra Mann, email message to author, July 12, 2022, quoted in Mathis, *Jesus among the Homeless*, 61.

community at its best. In 2004, Yvonne ministered in England to the predominately white and upper-class members of Holy Trinity Brompton at their Alpha Marriage and Prison Ministry conferences. She, along with other Christians from diverse nationalities and cultural backgrounds, broke ground for the development of a cross-cultural Christian community interceding at St. Paul's Church during J. John's "Just 10" revival. At the "Soul in the City" tent revival at Clapham Common that same summer, Yvonne and I served supper with Christians from every nationality and cultural background to thousands of souls that the Holy Spirit directed into that tent to hear Mike Pilavachi call them home to Jesus. These are some examples of the ways in which God continues to use Yvonne's personal history, social skills, and spiritual gifts to break down the walls of prejudice and build cross-cultural Christian community.

In 2005, I was honored to attend a Southern California Motion Picture Arts Council Award luncheon with Yvonne. At that event she received the Southern California Motion Picture Arts Council Life Time Charitable Achievement Award. As I sat at the table and listened to her speak, I became aware that God brought this saint of the church into my life from her Mississippi background; she has enriched my life by helping me understand how to override cultural barriers with the grace of God in order to help fulfill the great mission of the church: the Great Commission.[23]

Yvonnette still sings the black spirituals that she heard her mother sing to Jesus in her youth. She attended Christian churches in Mississippi where Scripture was revered as the word of God. Her deep relationship with Jesus as a child impacted her adult ministries.

She is a moderator each week on the "Fueled By Prayer" prayer line. In her own words, she "puts God in remembrance of His Word" citing Scriptures to demonstrate the effectiveness of praying in the name of Jesus:

23. DeFazio and Lathrop, *Creative Ways*, 24–25.

"And I will do whatever you ask in my name, so that the Father may be glorified in the Son. You may ask me for anything in my name, and I will do it" (John 14:13–14, NIV).

Yvonnette begins this weekly hour of prayer explaining that to pray in Jesus' name believers must "confess their sins," according to 1 John 1:9, because "if we confess our sins, he is faithful and just to forgive us our sins and purify us from all unrighteousness" (NIV).

She leads the intercessors in praise, worship, and Scripture reading each week, reminding them of Jesus' redemptive work: his innocent blood shed on Calvary for the forgiveness of all sin, emphasizing that through Jesus' death and resurrection, Christians have access to the Father and pray empowered by the Holy Spirit:

"The Spirit you received does not make you slaves, so that you live in fear again; rather, the Spirit you received brought about your adoption to sonship. And by him we cry, '*Abba*, Father'" (Rom 8:15 NIV, emphasis original).

Yvonnette, as a prayer warrior, stands faithfully on the word of God, guiding intercessors to pray as the Holy Spirit unites them in a fellowship with Jesus.

She welcomes anyone who needs prayer to call on Fridays at 9 p.m., eastern standard time. Dial 1-872-240-3412 and enter access code 332-085-709#.

RICHARD ADAMS

My grandmother lived to be a few short days from one hundred. Her faith in Jesus was everything to her. She was a fierce prayer warrior. If I brought prayer to her she would always say, "It will be around the world before we get off the phone." Here is one thing she taught me:

"Everyone has something to teach you even if it is a good example of what not to do."

She lived her faith and passed it on to her six kids and twenty-two grandchildren. Thank God for Sally

Plemons, my grandmother. Thank you, God, for the time I had with my grandmother.[24]

GREG BRUNET

My lifelong friend Jeanne DeFazio called me recently telling me she was collecting stories from people who prayed to receive Jesus as Lord and Savior. I recalled that over fifty years ago Steve Buskarin asked me to pray with him to receive Jesus while I was in my early twenties. I chose not to pray with him. Steve was a member of Trinity Tabernacle Church in Davis, California. I don't recall the details of the prayer, but I remember that Steve was a kindly and outgoing person always helping others. He managed apartments where I lived while a student at UC Davis. I enjoyed talking to him and we got into a conversation about God. I am not a religious person. I grew up in a family without traditional Christian values. We did not attend church. I listened to Steve talk about Jesus as Lord of His life because I could see that he tried to be a decent person. He told me that he wanted to be a missionary.

Jeanne said the Sinner's Prayer while listening to a friend who was a student at UC Davis. She recalls experiencing great joy after saying the prayer. I do not share her experience but always listen when she shares her faith in Jesus because I love her and realize her faith is important to her. And that is what friends do for each other. I tell her about what is important to me and she listens. That is why after over half a century we are still friends. Jeanne has my permission to include my story in this book. She asked for it so that people who did not pray the Sinner's Prayer when they had the opportunity would also be included in this book.[25]

---

24. Richard Adams, text message to author, July 12, 2024.
25. Greg Brunet, phone conversation with author, July 15, 2024.

The Journey Home
PEGGY VANEK-TITUS

When I was just a kid the west coast sound rocked me to sleep from a tiny radio. Too young to make the Summer of Love. Darn it. But we rarely travel in straight lines. My teenage years thrived under a one word banner ... HIPPIE! Individualism, free everything, and most of all my belief that allsoneallwasoneallisgodiamyouandyouaremeandweareacitaltogether. Highlight of my week was the local LRY (Liberal Religious Youth) meeting at the Unitarian Church. College called and sought out more history in St. Paul, MN. I had recently been presented with the Gospel. You know the one: "I am the Way, the Truth, the Life. No one comes to the Father except through ME." You know the one—heaven, hell. Trouble was, "head" got it; "heart" was still doin' pitter-pats over universalism. I mean, light is light, right? Wrong. Darn it.

West coast bliss to my rescue. Six members of The Christian World Liberation Front are on the road; they have got their RV revved up and rockin' out the best recruiting sites in the nation, and I am smack dab in the center of one of these hot spots. They rolled up to the Bethel College Campus in the Twin Cities and I am one giddy girl ... a FAN! (of a ministry, no less). I am familiar with their Right On newspaper, and I am convinced that if I am going to identify with Christianity at all, it's going to have to be within the context of this group. I mean the name itself—Christian World Liberation Front—oh my gosh. The mysterious, radical, exhilarating, connected to the truth. They made Christianity palatable. And God only knew I needed to eat some of His grub. In recent months I had taken copies of their newspaper and traced pictures of some of their members over and over again with my fingers; whispering, "You're family, you're family." So here I am, seated cross-legged on the floor; every cell in my body extended for their chapel chat. One woman takes the mic. There is a hush. "It's do or die!" Her dark eyes penetrate chapel light. "Who is willing to lay it on the line? Who is willing to come to the front lines? I know one person is! I know Peggy Vanek

Titus is willing!" Recruit? Who, me? To Berkeley? Take me NOW! I beamed and blushed. The Children of God had tried to snag me a year earlier in Nashville. COG . . . zero . . . The Front . . . SCORE! Liberation happens.

Fast forward . . . school's out for summer! I make my way back down south to work toward a one-way (pun intended) trip to Berkeley. Berkeley. Now there's some history for ya. And I had decided not to make it a summer internship; oh no! I was moving, sight unseen, across the country. Really? Someone and many thereafter have said that we often see more clearly with the eyes of our heart. Well, keep on pumping, baby. The IHOP griddle was greasing it down; stuffed puffed cheeks full of white toast, white grits, and white pancakes; "mush mouths" washing it all down with coffee and sweet tea chasers.

I wiped those sticky sweet syrupy tables down as my apron jingle-jangled its way to a plane ticket. The black-and-white population I served every morning would soon be replaced by every rainbow complexion, and the stuffed puffed cheeks would be full of whole grain everything; natural peanut butter, raw skim milk and Tillamook cheddar. Yum. Some months later in Berkeley, I would be so proud and pleased with myself growing tiny crops of mung beans and alfalfa sprouts in a darkened hall closet.

When my plane landed in San Francisco and my feet touched down on California soil, my soul whispered, "I'm home."

Now it was off to meet the family! There was CWLF founder, "Daddy" Jack Sparks, the whole state of California serving up Mother Earth, Sky and Sun, and my brothers and sisters from every state imaginable and other nations as well.[26]

---

26. Peggy Vanek-Titus, email message to author, Mar. 23, 2022, quoted in DeFazio, *Christian World Liberation*, 37–38.

The Journey Home

JOZY POLLOCK

In 1982, a relationship I had with a man I had found through a psychic's predictions brought me to the end of my rope. I called a friend named Mike who had accepted Jesus after years of drinking and drugging. I told him that I had had enough torment and I wanted peace. He told me that, if I prayed the sinner's prayer, I could have peace. I did not feel like a sinner, because I had always been a good friend and looked out for others. I was the unpaid psychiatrist to my friends who were going through traumas. I prayed the sinner's prayer, but pleaded with the Lord not to turn me into a Jesus freak. I went to a Chi Coltrane Christian concert at the Vineyard.[27] She was talking about being "born again," explaining that it was a step of faith, and that salvation is assured even if you are not feeling it. This was exactly where I was in my walk. I found out she had a Bible study at her home, and I attended. I told her how I was feeling. She prayed with me and laid hands on me. I started speaking in tongues. Suddenly, I had a huge hunger and thirst for God. It took me a long time to submit to the Holy Spirit, but, after I gave up my will, I had peace. When I was water baptized in a home in Bel Air, I fell in love with Jesus and became invisible to men. I needed to build my relationship with Jesus. I have been celibate since being saved. This was God's shield.[28]

LINDA LOCKHART

I ended a relationship. I had plans for my future. One day, I shut the door in the living room of my apartment. As I entered the kitchen, a beam of light shined through the window. I walked into the beam of light, which was Jesus' presence, and I raised my hands in worship and I said, "You got me." Looking back, I understand that my

---

27. Chi Coltrane had a notable hit with her song "Thunder and Lightning," but was now singing for Jesus with songs such as "Go Like Elijah."

28. DeFazio and Spencer, *Redeeming the Screens*, 66–67.

own plans for the future were not God's plans and, in retrospect, I saw His hand of protection over my life. I was on the floor crying. I made a phone call to a friend and said, "I don't know what's going on, I love you, you will understand."

At that point, I reached out by telephone to Marilyn Hickey Ministries and a prayer partner led me in the salvation prayer to receive Jesus as my Lord and Savior. For a year after that, I listened to Marilyn Hickey teaching on television and she asked, at the close of a program, if anyone wanted to receive Jesus. I prayed once again to receive Him as my Lord and Savior. She walked me through the beginning of my "born again" life. Shortly after that, I met Pastor Winn and was baptized at Gordon College.[29]

WILMA FAYE MATHIS

At a very early age, I was nurtured under a praying and godly grandmother who taught me the value of prayer and that started me on my journey to growing in the knowledge of God. I was baptized and received Jesus as my Lord and Savior at the age of 14. Growing up in church, while dealing with life during my youth/young adult life, had its challenges. I went through many highs and lows and then experienced a period of such devastation that I contemplated taking my own life. It was at the point of survival that God led me to know, "I have allowed you not to die, that you may cause others to live." Through this experience, I knew for certain the call of God was upon my life. I totally surrendered and I am still here to tell the story. Thank God the prayers of my grandmother have no expiration date.[30]

---

29. Linda Lockhart, phone conversation with author, June 26, 2024.
30. Wilma Faye Mathis, email message to author, June 26, 2024.

The Journey Home

LINDA BAIR SMITH

My story began when I was seven years old. A friend invited me to a neighborhood Bible Club where I prayed to ask Jesus into my life. It was very meaningful to me, but my family did not go to church and we moved soon after that. A few years later we started going to a denominational church. I liked going to church. I knew we celebrated Christmas when Jesus was born and Easter when Jesus died for us and rose to heaven, but I did not know we could know Him. I thought he was up in heaven watching us to see how we did (if we could make it to heaven). I did not know that because he rose from the dead, He is alive now, and we can actually know Jesus as a person, like a friend—until, as a senior in college, I went with my mother to a Full Gospel meeting. The love of God was very real in the room and with two messages in tongues with interpretation (which my mother and I had never heard before). I knew that not only was Jesus in that room, but He was talking to me. He said, "Trust Me and follow Me." I said, "OK." My life has never been the same since.[31]

MARTHA REYES

In 1972, our mother decided to move to California where some of her relatives resided. Rearing four children by herself was no easy matter, and her relatives were willing to help. Puerto Rico, as part of the United States, is a bi-cultural and a bilingual country. It shares the best of both worlds: the opportunities and possibilities of being part of a developed nation and a deeply rooted sense of connectivity with third-world countries in Latin America. For this reason, I integrated rapidly with Hispanics in the United States and have been part of the United States Hispanic subculture from day one.

---

31. Linda Bair Smith, email message to author, June 26, 2024.

In California, while working as a lounge singer and musician, I was also a full-time student of psychology at California State University, thanks to the help of some large student loans. While finishing a master's degree in psychology, through the efforts of Campus Crusade for Christ, I came to the Lord and immediately began searching for God's divine purpose in my life.[32]

MIDORI ARIMOTO

Michael P. Grace II took me to several Los Angeles Christian events in the 1980s and 1990s. I am familiar with the Sinner's Prayer because at these events there were altar calls where people attending were encouraged to come to the altar or the front of a room and pray to receive Jesus as Lord and Savior. I prayed to receive Jesus at one of these meetings. Jeanne DeFazio organized a missionary tour to Israel for Mr. Grace. I went on that tour and was baptized in the Jordan River as a Christian in 1987. This experience really encouraged my faith. I have been involved in New Age beliefs since that time but I continue to pray as a Christian and ask Christian friends to pray for me and my family.[33]

UNITED STATES SENATE CHAPLAIN LLOYD OGILVIE

It is not surprising that I am deeply committed to Bible studies and small fellowship groups meeting in the secular world. I became a Christian as a freshman in college. An informal Bible study and discussion group met down the hall from my dormitory room. After listening in on the communication of a dynamic quality of Christianity, I made my commitment to Christ. The group nurtured me in my first steps of following the Savior. Since then,

---

32. DeFazio and Spencer, *Redeeming the Screens*, 91–92.
33. Midori Arimoto, text message to author, July 15, 2024.

I have never been without my own group of covenant brothers and sisters who meet to share the adventure and accountability of discipleship.

That's the reason that, during fifty-five years of ministry, I have felt called to equip and encourage people to live out their faith in government, business, education, entertainment, various professions, and in their families. In addition to caring for them personally, I have been committed to developing Bible studies and small groups to provide mutual support and strength for them to be faithful and effective disciples.

Most people work about 160,000 hours during their lifetime. Those who take few vacations and work after hours will work about 200,000 hours. A housewife will work more than 290,000! Work can be a false god and the object of worship. The challenge for most Christians is to bring meaning to their work rather than making their work the primary meaning of their lives. To do that, they need other believers with whom they can meet consistently to deepen their faith through study of the Scriptures, sharing of hopes and needs, and prayer for each other. There should be no solo flights for those who are committed to Christ, who need fresh grace for daily living under the plumb line of His righteousness, who need courage to seek His guidance for crucial decisions, and who long to communicate their faith, hope, and love to others who also struggle in the strain and stress of secular life.

In each of the churches I have served as pastor, I have witnessed firsthand the power of Christians meeting together in the business community, in colleges and universities, in the movie industry, and in homes and neighborhoods. The basic purpose of these dynamic fellowship groups has been to enable people to press on with wisdom, vision, courage, and supernatural power.

One of the most challenging areas to serve is in government, particularly in Washington, DC. I have come to believe that being an elected member of the Congress or to serve on his or her staff is a very high calling. When I was elected to serve as the 61st United States Senate Chaplain, I felt that my primary purpose was to encourage our leaders and their staffs to grow in their relationship with the Lord, the Sovereign of our Nation, and to seek His will in the monumental responsibilities and soul-sized decisions entrusted to them. In addition to opening the Senate each day in prayer, my privilege was to be an intercessor for the Senators and their families, a trusted prayer partner, and a faithful spiritual counselor.

During my years as chaplain (1995–2003), I had five major Bible studies each week: the Senators met on Thursday, the Senators' spouses on Tuesday, the Chiefs of Staff on Wednesday, and two staff groups, one on Tuesday and the other on Friday. The great Scriptures of the Old and New Testament were shared in an effort to empower the Senators and their staffs both personally and professionally. In addition, small groups were formed in offices for in-depth reflection and prayer. These groups were called the H.O.S.I.—the Holy Order of Senate Intercessors. Leaders of these groups were trained; materials for discussion were provided. These spiritually empowered, morally rooted, ethically focused men and women meet together for inspired introspection and vision, and then press on with integrity, imagination, and the impelling inspiration of the Holy Spirit in the crucial realms of responsibility where they have been divinely deployed to serve.

I saw my role as chaplain to be non-political, non-partisan and non-sectarian. With our heritage as Americans, there never can be a separation of God and state! I was deeply honored to follow Dr. Richard Halverson in the chaplaincy and to be succeeded by Dr. Barry Black, both truly great spiritual enablers of those who are called to serve in government.[34]

---

34. Lloyd Ogilvie, interview by email with author, July 2012, quoted in DeFazio and Lathrop, *Creative Ways*, 17–20.

CONCLUSION

JEANNE DEFAZIO

This collection of Christian testimonies identifies the varied and unique ways the Holy Spirit touches the lives of nonbelievers bringing each one home to Jesus as Lord and Savior. Some of these stories describe those who came to Jesus when they needed physical healing. Others turned to Jesus because mystical paths did not bring peace or happiness. We are all prodigal sons and daughters. Each of us have experienced heartache and pain from looking for God's love in all the wrong places. God, like the father in the gospel account, has unconditional love for his children and forgives and welcomes home those who repent for straying:

> And he said, "There was a man who had two sons. And the younger of them said to his father, 'Father, give me the share of property that is coming to me.' And he divided his property between them. Not many days later, the younger son gathered all he had and took a journey into a far country, and there he squandered his property in reckless living. And when he had spent everything, a severe famine arose in that country, and he began to be in need. So he went and hired himself out to one of the citizens of that country, who sent him into his fields to feed pigs. And he was longing to be fed with the pods that the pigs ate, and no one gave him anything.
>
> But when he came to himself, he said, "How many of my father's hired servants have more than enough bread, but I perish here with hunger! I will arise and go to my father, and I will say to him, 'Father, I have sinned against heaven and before you. I am no longer worthy to be called your son. Treat me as one of your hired servants.'" And he arose and came to his father.
>
> But while he was still a long way off, his father saw him and felt compassion, and ran and embraced him and kissed him. And the son said to him, "Father, I have sinned against heaven and before you. I am no longer worthy to be called your son." But the father said to his servants, "Bring quickly the best robe, and put it on him,

and put a ring on his hand, and shoes on his feet. And bring the fattened calf and kill it, and let us eat and celebrate. For this my son was dead, and is alive again; he was lost, and is found." And they began to celebrate.

Now his older son was in the field, and as he came and drew near to the house, he heard music and dancing. And he called one of the servants and asked what these things meant. 'Your brother has come,' he replied, 'and your father has killed the fattened calf because he has him back safe and sound.'

The older brother became angry and refused to go in. So his father went out and pleaded with him.... And he said to him, "My son, you are always with me, and all that is mine is yours. It was fitting to celebrate and be glad, for this your brother was dead, and is alive; he was lost, and is found." (Luke 15:11–29, 31–32 NIV)

The incredible joy I felt when I received Jesus as my Lord and Savior as a young adult is one of my favorite memories. That is why I say the Sinner's Prayer often:

> Thank You for dying on the cross for my sins. I open the door of my life and receive You as my Savior and Lord. Thank You for forgiving my sins and giving me eternal life. Take control of the throne of my life. Make me the kind of person You want me to be.

When I first said the Sinner's Prayer, I did not realize how challenging my life would be. Over the past fifty years, the prayer has become very meaningful to me: I repeat "Lord Jesus, I need You" often because I understand how much I need Jesus just to survive. I thank Jesus for dying on the cross for my sins because I am fully aware that I fall short of the glory of God and need his forgiveness. I receive Jesus as my Lord and Savior repeatedly because without his Lordship over my life I would be totally lost. I beg Jesus to take control of the throne of my life so I don't totally mess everything up. I ask Jesus to make me the kind of person he wants me to be because I really get tired of my human nature. I praise and thank Jesus daily for the Holy Spirit's presence and God's mercy, which have sustained me through my adult life. I am so grateful to Jesus for loving me.

About the Authors

Julia C. Davis has an EdM from the Harvard Graduate School of Education and an EdM from Bouve College of Health Sciences at Northeastern University. She has held teaching certificates in New York, Massachusetts, and the District of Columbia and has been certified as an assistant principal and as an assistant special education supervisor. Julia has taught in the public and private sector in community-based programs, including METCO, Summer STEP opportunities for underrepresented populations in science and technology, and Head Start. She has served as a member of Parent's Advocacy Group for Massachusetts, as a supporter of Free Appropriate Public Education (FAPE), and in helping to mainstream special education students. She has taught pre-K through twelfth grade, Adult Nonreaders, Limited English Language Learners, and GED preparation courses. Julia taught internationally as an undergraduate exchange student in a special education program based in Newnham on Severn in Gloucestershire, England, which operated under the auspices of Antioch College in Ohio. Julia and her husband Dan have three children and three grandchildren. They attend the International Family Church in North Reading, Massachusetts.

Jeanne DeFazio is a former SAG/AFTRA (Screen Actors Guild / American Federation of Television and Radio Artists) actress of Spanish-Italian descent, who played supporting parts in theater, movies, and television series, then served the marginalized in the drama of real life. She became a teacher of second-language-learner children in the barrios of San Diego. She completed a BA in history at the University of California, Davis, an MAR at Gordon-Conwell Theological Seminary, and a certificate for teachers of English learners at Cal State. From 2009 to the present, she has served as an Athanasian teaching scholar at Gordon-Conwell's Boston campus, the Campus for Urban Ministerial Education.

Bibliography

Bernstein, James A. *Surprised by Christ: My Journey from Judaism to Orthodox Christianity.* Lomar, CA: Conciliar, 2008.

Cru. "Four Spiritual Laws: 'The Basics' Series." Campus Ministry Today, 2007. https://campusministry.org/docs/tools/FourSpiritualLaws.pdf.

Davis, Julia C., and Jeanne C. DeFazio. *An Artistic Tribute to Harriet Tubman.* Eugene, OR: Resource, 2021.

DeFazio, Jeanne C., ed. *Berkeley Street Theatre: How Improvisation and Street Theater Emerged as a Christian Outreach to the Culture of the Time.* Eugene, OR: Wipf & Stock, 2017.

———, ed. *The Commission: The God Who Calls Us to Be a Voice during a Pandemic, Wildfires, and Racial Violence.* Eugene, OR: Wipf & Stock, 2021.

———. *Finding a Better Way.* Eugene, OR: Wipf & Stock, 2021.

———. *Keeping the Dream Alive: A Reflection on the Art of Harriet Lorence Nesbitt.* Eugene, OR: Resource, 2019.

DeFazio, Jeanne C., and John Lathrop, eds. *Creative Ways to Build Christian Community.* Eugene, OR: Wipf & Stock, 2013.

DeFazio, Jeanne C., and William David Spencer, eds. *Empowering English Language Learners: Successful Strategies of Christian Educators.* House of Prisca and Aquila. Eugene, OR: Wipf & Stock, 2018.

———, eds. *Redeeming the Screens.* House of Prisca and Aquila. Eugene, OR: Wipf & Stock, 2016.

Flowers, Teresa, and Jeanne C. DeFazio. *How to Have an Attitude of Gratitude on the Night Shift.* Eugene, OR: Resource, 2014.

Mathis, Wilma Faye. *Jesus among the Homeless.* House of Prisca and Aquila. Wipf & Stock, Eugene, OR: 2023.

www.ingramcontent.com/pod-product-compliance
Lightning Source LLC
Chambersburg PA
CBHW072037060426
42449CB00010BA/2305